A Quick Procedure for Language Cleanup before Senior Technical Review
©2015 Christa Bedwin
Additional print and eBook copies can be purchased through Amazon.
Library and Archives Canada Cataloguing in Publication
ISBN: book: 978-0-9918976-9-8
       e-book: 978-1-987990-02-7
Bedwin, Christa, 1974 –, author
A Quick Procedure for Language Cleanup before Senior Technical Review / Christa Bedwin

www.solarosatech.com

SOLA
ROSA
This book was produced by Sola Rosa Publishing, Canada.
Our mission is to publish only books that help people feel good or help them live better.
Layout: Raaj Chandran.
Editing: Patricia McIsaac.

With thanks to the many senior engineers, scientists, and business people who shared their concerns and mentorship strategies with me in the development of this book.

Your feedback and thoughts are welcome! E-mail me at christabedwin@solarosatech.com.

A Quick Procedure for
Language Cleanup
before
Senior Technical Review

CHRISTA BEDWIN
B. Ed., B.Sc., CYT

SOLA
ROSA

Contents

Expanded information (e.g. word lists) is available in "Client-Pleasing Reports and Communications" available from the author on www.amazon.com.

Purpose & Overview

It can be impossible to review a document for its technical aspects when the English is muddled.

Ideally, English language polishing should happen before documents reach senior reviewers, but due to scheduling crunches, this often fails to happen, and the technical reviewer ends up needing to decipher the English before they can even begin on the technical detail.

This course is a procedure that has worked well for me to speed-edit countless reports "at the last minute." The aim of the course is to help you refine a procedure that works well for the documents that you are faced with in the final stages before they go to the client.

What are the highest-impact things that you can do in a short period of time? Your objectives are:

- clear comprehension for technical review
- good quality English
- easy access/comprehension of the information by the client
- logical organization
- good aesthetics

Having these steps separated out into this procedure may also help you identify team members who might take on roles to reduce the schedule-crunched workload, and may help you to develop procedures that will work to reduce the last-minute problems in your reporting chain. (See the troubleshooting appendix.)

A cost-saving and effective alternative is sometimes to simply develop a relationship with a freelance editor. Experiment with this – if you find the right person, it can decrease your costs and stress level, increase client satisfaction, and help you meet deadlines well.

If your department does not have access to an editor, then consider identifying someone in your group with strong language skills, and seek further training and mentorship to develop that person's skills, customized to reducing the particular issues within your own group. A common pattern within consulting firms has been to assume that project administrators or coordinators should be document editors, however, these people are often not as skilled in language excellence as is assumed, and this book can help reduce the gap somewhat to increase skills and trust in the process.

However, these individuals may not understand the technical detail well enough to do a strong substantive edit, and the role again falls to the senior technical reviewer.

Note that this course only addresses the language edit. The document must also be reviewed for:

- technical accuracy
- liability protection

Assessing the Document: The Ten-Minute Editor

This checklist should take only about ten minutes to do a sweep of a document and decide what the highest priority items for fixing are. Use this checklist to help you avoid getting distracted by niggling issues while you do a high-level assessment to organize your thoughts, your tasks, and your time.

Premium Tip

Stylin' it Old School
Have a note pad near your computer and take pen and paper notes as you scan through this checklist. The process of having physical paper beside your computer helps you to organize your thoughts better than trying to keep everything on-screen.

1. Organization & Appearance

The single highest-impact thing that you can do for a document is to make sure that the most important points are standing right out at the front of paragraphs where the client can easily see them. (Authors sometimes bury the most important points in the middle of paragraphs, writing along in stream-of-consciousness mode.)

How the report looks is the first impression clients get of your professionalism.

Check the Table of Contents to make sure that the information marches along in a logical way and has a balance (in pages per section) that matches the importance of each type of information.

2. Solid Introduction & Conclusions

Does the author explain right up front why the reader/client needs to read this report and what they will get out of it, giving enough of a summary to explain without presuming on past communications?

By the end of the document, does the writer give the appropriate conclusions that were promised? Does the reader feel that they have reached a satisfactory end point with solid back-up of information?

Premium Tip

The Best is Last

By the end of a document, writers have normally thought their way around to the essence of what they really have to say.

If you are entering a new report without knowing anything about it, start by reading the conclusion. It is often the most coherent piece of writing in an unedited report.

3. Sentences, Paragraphs, & Punctuation

Sentences should be simple and straightforward. Paragraphs should contain only one idea each. Bulleted lists are 10 to 20 times faster for readers to scan and understand than heavy paragraphs when you have parallel information.

Are there any persistent errors in punctuation, or general repeated sloppy inattention to punctuation? Readers can be distracted by inconsistently punctuated lists or confused by oddly punctuated sentences.

4. Trash

A variety of words can be completely discarded or replaced with much shorter phrases. This can be quick to do with search and replace, or a macro.

5. "To Be" Verbs: Passive & Clunky Sentences

Passive language uses forms of "to be": is, am, are, was, were, has been, have been, be, being, been. Trim fat from sentences by getting rid of passive "to be" verbs and equation sentences.

6. Particular Persistent Issues

Many writers have a few persistent, repeated issues with certain words and grammatical structures. Once identified, these can often be hunt-and-fixed quite quickly using Word's "Search and Replace" function.

Use Formatting to Read a Hard Report

If you are faced with a wall of bad writing and you have it in electronic form, try these tricks based on typesetting and readability principles to make your life easier.

Premium Tips

1. Change the Font

If a manuscript has been handed to you in a difficult-to-read font, change the font to one that is easier for you to read.

Verdana, Arial, Calibri, Times New Roman, Courier, and Comic Sans are typical font choices for readability's sake, but you can choose whatever suits you best. When you are finished editing, as required, you can return it to another font.

2. Increase The Spacing Between Lines

It gives your eye more space and allows you to read more quickly.

3. Decrease the Column Width

This can increase the ease of reading dense text. If you have used Tip 2 already, you might not need this one.

4. Untangle Complicated Sentences

Insert a carriage return after each sentence to read them more easily. (This greatly reduces the brain-boggling factor.)

This really helps to untangle the ideas and edit the sentences to be more simple, more quickly. When you view the ideas when they are laid out as if in a bulleted list, it is easy to see when ideas are:

- out of order
- repeated
- tangled

You can compress the sentences into paragraphs again after you have processed them.

A note from your team:

This procedure guide is intended to streamline and speed up your process. You may not want to monkey with the formatting if the document has already been formatted in a company template, as it may cause your formatters to need to redo it.

Over the years admins have very often had to redo report formatting because seniors have made small, silly mistakes that cause hours of extra work later. One such silly timewaster is to correct typos in the table of contents – it must be corrected in the headers in the report, not in the formatted table of contents. When seniors have done that one 5-second action, admins had 3 more hours of work. Talk to your whole team to find glitches in the process. **Administrators often hesitate to speak up about what is not working in the process. As a senior reviewer, it falls to you to seek out the knowledge that can improve the process for the team.**

Example: An Unsafe Paragraph of Safety Instructions

This example shows how to use the Premium Tips to edit this paragraph.

While on the Gabu site, apply salt to any areas that ice up. Ice clampons are provided for use on site visitors' boots. Ensure that handrails are available along icy paths. Maintain situational awareness at all times. Be vigilant of potential oncoming vehicles in front, behind, and to both sides. If you are underwater, also be aware of dangers from above and below. Present a strong posture as you move through the danger zone. A strong posture and determined gaze can deter muggers.

It's a mess, yet a not uncommon schmozzle for a consulting firm. Someone has compiled a bunch of safety instructions from other projects, formatted them so they think it looks cool, and called them the safety documentation for a new project. Let's apply:

- Premium Tip 1: Fix up the font.
- Premium Tip 4: Add carriage returns.
- Premium Tip 2: Add spacing between lines.

Which gives us:

- While on the Gabu site, apply salt to any areas that ice up.

- Ice clampons are provided for use on site visitors' boots.

- Ensure that handrails are available along icy paths.

- Maintain situational awareness at all times.

- Be vigilant of potential oncoming vehicles in front, behind, and to both sides.

- If you are underwater, also be aware of dangers from above and below.

- Present a strong posture as you move through the danger zone.

- A strong posture and determined gaze can deter muggers.

Now it is easy to see that:

- Some of these points are about ice.
- Others are about situational awareness.
- They are not written with parallel structure.
- One seems to be irrelevant – the Gabu site does not involve diving for pipe repair.
  (Unfortunately, it is quite common for people to copy and paste irrelevant parts from other projects.)

By grouping them, it is now simple to also reduce the amount of words and put it into a question-answer format for easier reading. Compare how easily you grasp what is below compared to the original paragraph. Imagine how much greater that impact is for field workers!

Safety at the Gabu site:

Ice:	- Salt areas that ice up.
	- Give visitors ice boot clampons.
	- Provide and maintain handrails along icy paths.
Situational awareness:	- Be vigilant for vehicles from all directions.
	- Present a strong posture and determined gaze to deter muggers.

ORGANIZATION & APPEARANCE

The client's first impression of your professionalism will be how your document looks and feels. There are several very fast strategies that can make a big difference.

Check the Table of Contents

Review the Table of Contents. This is an easy place to start, it's important, and you can quickly familiarize yourself with the document.

- Do the headings reflect the balance of the important information that should be in the report?

- Are all the important pieces covered in sufficient detail?

- Is there any topic that has too much detail?

- Is the content covered in a sensible order?

- Do the heading levels reflect a logical hierarchy of information?

- Do all the headings make sense (spell out all acronyms, as they are clouds to readers)?

Quick & Dirty Methods: Break up long paragraphs

1–2 minutes per page

The way we read has changed with the advent of the internet. Important points should be at the front of paragraphs, and paragraphs should be short.

- Long blocks of text are hard to read. Insert line breaks.

- Bulleted lists are magic. It is 10 to 20 times faster to process a bulleted list of parallel information, than that same list crammed into a paragraph.

- Watch for long sentences (signalled often by semi-colons) and break them up into two or turn them into bulleted lists.

Premium Tip

Get Some Head Room

If you are faced with long, dense reams of text, it is often a lot easier to edit it by inserting a line return after every sentence. Then it's easy to see what is out of order, what's too long, what's repeated, and what's nonsense. After you clean it up, you can remove the line breaks again (usually to find a much smaller and cleaner paragraph than you started with).

INTRODUCTION & CONCLUSION

The introduction and conclusion are essential parts of every document, even if they are only a sentence in an e-mail. They are often the first pieces that are read, and contain the essential information.

They are the foundations that hold the document strong or leave it oozing shapelessly. Even if all else is mush, these two pieces must be solid.

A missing introduction starts off a confusing read for the reader.

A missing conclusion feels like an unfinished job.

Introduction

The introduction should introduce any reader to the purpose of the document so that they comfortably feel that they know where this document is going and why it was written.

Occasionally, writers wrapped up in the job may forget to orient their readers. Do not assume every reader was on the phone with you and the client five minutes ago.

Assume that readers and clients are busy, tired, and stressed out – they may completely forget details you recently told them aloud.

Check that the introduction:

- tells **who**, **what**, **when**, **where**, **why** and **how** this document came about

- does not contain extra useless distracting info. It only needs the key points.

The purpose of the introduction is so the reader knows what value they will get from reading the report.

The introduction is not merely a formality. You write an introduction as a courtesy to your readers because there is special information that we, their favourite service provider, have collected for a specific purpose.

Conclusion

Readers and reviewers will often flip to the conclusion to find out what the document was about. A well-done conclusion makes an excellent executive summary (though it is nice to reword it somewhat to avoid being obvious). Readers count on it to be the place that authors will get to the point after they have meandered around doing their reasoning and calculations.

It is absolutely essential that the conclusion does deliver the essential technical points that the client needs to know. What did we find out? What are your recommendations? Why do you say that? Are next steps needed?

SENTENCES, PARAGRAPHS, & PUNCTUATION

The shape of the words on the page has a huge influence on readability. In the high-pressure world of industry, clients or colleagues can get very annoyed by seemingly trivial issues such as inconsistent punctuation.

As well, it is essential to highlight the important points by placing them at the fronts of paragraphs. If appropriate, perhaps bold leading topic sentences. Do not bury important ideas in the middle of paragraphs or dense pages of text.

Yes, a paragraph can be one sentence.

When reviewing in a rush, you can revolutionize the client's reading experience even by the simple measure of finding somewhere in a wallish page of text to insert a bulleted list for some parallel items.

Premium Tip

Readability Science
The people in the highest places tend to be the most easily distracted by small errors. As the stress level goes up, reading ability goes down.
The following items help text to be more readable:

- short sentences
- short paragraphs
- narrower columns
- defined spaces on the page

PARTICULAR ISSUES

Certain writers have easily identifiable issues. Once you sort out the procedure to fix each kind of error, you can often get quite speedy with these kind of fixes.

Quick & Dirty Methods: Run PerfectIt software

20 minutes for a long document

http://www.intelligentediting.com

If you deal with reports that have words that are often capitalized and hyphenated differently, such as reports with multiple authors, or if you have long documents that need acronym lists, then the following piece of software is well worth it. It costs less than one chargeable hour per user.

It is a very fast way to make sure tables and figures are all named and listed properly, and that many ragged edges are properly cleaned up. And it creates an acronym list!

Note that you **do** need to apply your intelligence to accept or reject its suggestions – such as using "long-term" hyphenated as an adjective, or "long term" unhyphenated as a noun, but it's a wonderful timesaver.

Premium Tip

Preventing Consistency Issues
Create a style sheet with spellings and hyphenations of commonly used words at the outset of a project. Distribute the style sheet to the entire team and be firm with the expectation that all team members follow it.

Quick & Dirty Methods: Search and destroy chronic or persistent distracting errors

2–15 minutes each

Every writer has certain chronic problem words. Some of us have more than others, and some errors are a lot easier to find than others.

When you identify these ones, hunt and fix them throughout the document. See the "trash" section for other common culprits.

Common confused words include:
- affect, effect, impact, result
- comprise (better to replace with a suitable word, as even if you correct a wrong use of comprise, this is likely to be wrongenated at a future review by someone)
- discreet, discrete
- farther, further
- fewer, less
- lose, loose
- threw, throw, through, though
- where, were, we're, wear, ware

Fixing Common Errors

1. Adjectives are singular

Adjectives take a singular form. For example, "there were 89 **cow** bells ringing in the **flower** meadow. Many ESL (English Second Language, or third or fourth or fifth language!) writers use plural adjectives. Though there are **cows** and **flowers** in the meadow, we write **cow bells**, not cows bells, and **flower meadow**, not flowers meadow.

The fix: Find individual problems, then use search and replace to fix all other cases of each one.

2. "The" and "a"

Many ESL writers omit the words "the" and "a" or add them in the wrong place. Keep an eye on this.

3. Correct metric units

Metric units always come after a space. There should never be a hyphen between a number and its unit.

Though you might not care in your group, your client readers often care to have it done correctly, so this is important to fix. And it's easy!

- Search for "km" and replace with " km" (space km).
- Search for "0m" and replace with "0 m" (0 space m). In rapid succession, then search for 1m replace with 1 m, 2m replace with 2 m, 3m replace with 3 m, and so on.

 Use a hard space (shift + ctrl + space) to avoid the unit breaking across the line after the number. Some people have written macros to fix all of those.

Polishing for Nicer Reading

There are certain red flags that show where you can make easy streamlining improvements in the writing.

Red Flag: Of the, for the

If you highlight everywhere that "of the" or "for the" appears, you can often find sentences that can be smoothed and rewritten with fewer words.

Red Flag: Semi-colons

Semi-colons can be a red flag for wordy writing and can often be annihilated. Change those sentences to two sentences or rewrite more clearly, which also almost always reduces the words.

Red Flag: –ing and –tion words

–ing

He was in the running. He was running. He was a running man. Is "running" a noun, a verb, or an adjective? If you are a native English speaker this might be easy to figure out, but –ing words can cause confusion. You can often make sentences more clear by replacing –ing words.

–tion

–tion words are often verbs that have been turned into nouns, requiring another verb to be added (messy and heavy).

- Consolidation can be changed to consolidate.
- Utilization can be reduced to utilize, and even better, to use.

What would you change enumeration to?

Red Flag: Negativity

Negatives cause a pause in the reading, muddy up the tone of writing, and do not develop relationships with your clients. It's a well-researched fact that people do not read, or hear, the word "not." They will often miss the word "not" and do the thing you suggest (which is actually the thing you do not suggest). So if you say "do not hesitate to call," they may hesitate to call. Suppose I ask you not to think of red apples? What do you do?

Instead of "Do not hesitate to contact us if you have questions," which does leave a bit of a pause in there whether you meant to or not, consider using:

- "We will be pleased to address any questions that you may have."
- "Contact us if you have any questions."

It's shorter, and leaves off the negative. It leaves your reader/client on a slightly more positive note.

Double negatives are usually not needed either. "This was not incorrect" is one example of a construction that shows up in documents. "The effects were not inconsiderable" is another. Search for "not" in the document, and consider if it's a "not" that is really needed or if you could smoothe out the tangle of nots by writing it another way.

Red Flag: Which and that

Which and that are commonly mis-used in writing and can change the meaning. Do a search for "which" in the document to quickly find out if this problem is prevalent.

In Canada, the general rule is that if you can use "that" instead of "which," do. As well, a comma usually appears before "which."

Exercise 1: Quick and Dirty Fixes and Red Flags

Apply just the quick and dirty fixes, and look for the red flags suggested above to make this document dramatically better.

BACKGROUND AND PROJECT DESCRIPTION

This report documents construction activities and construction quality assurance (CQA) completed for the expansion of the ACME Mine Tailings Storage Facility (TSF).

Project Description

ACME Mining and Metals (ACME) operates the ACME Mine located approximately 2 miles south of Area 51; in Conspiracy County, Nevada. The impoundment is operated by spigoting slurried fine mill tailings into the TSF using thin layer sub-aerial deposition to promote drying and densification of the tailings. The impoundment is a geomembrane-lined facility from which water is removed and recycled back to the mill for re-use.

The ACME TSF was designed to be constructed in seven stages. Stage 1 was substantially completed in December of 2005, Stage 2 was completed in September 2007, and Stage 3 was completed in November 2009. ACME completed construction of the fourth stage of development, Stages 4A and 4B, in September, 2011.

The Stage 4A expansion began in October 2009 and added approximately 3.0 million square feet of lined basin area to the existing TSF, and increased the dam height above the Stage 3 crest elevation by approximately 24 feet in the supernatant pool and transition areas; new embankment was also added to the west and east legs of the dam adjacent to the expansion of the basin.

Stage 4B construction followed Stage 4A construction with a winter shut-down during the 2010/2011 winter; The Stages 4A and 4B expansions combined added between approximately 30.4 million to 34.1 million tons of additional tailings storage capacity; with the range based on using either the originally assumed average density of 83 pounds per cubic foot (pcf) or a higher density of 93 pcf more recently inferred through surveys and field testing.

The key components constructed during Stage 4 included: construction of a staged temporary stormwater diversion ditch and retention pond north of the Stage 4 basin area; the placement of earth and rock fill in the dam; the installation of High Density polyethylene (HDPE) geomembrane liner in the impoundment basin area and upstream slope of the dam in the supernatant pool area; the installation of the underdrain piping system above the HDPE liner system in the basin; the extension of the gravity decant system on the upstream slope of the dam; extensions to the crest drains on the additional embankment legs added on the east and west ends, and relocation of the tailings spigoting system from the Stage 3 to the Stage 4 dam crest and basin perimeter. Construction of the Stage 4 expansion occurred from June 2010 to September 2011. Throughout this report, Stage 4 will refer to all work associated with both Stage 4A and 4B.

The dam and impoundment have been designed and constructed in accordance with Nevada Administrative Code (NAC) Chapter 445A and Water Pollution Control Permit NEV-0000 as administered by the Nevada Division of Environmental Protection (NDEP) Bureau of Mining Regulation and Reclamation, and in accordance with NAC Chapter 535 and Dam Permit J-000 as administered by the Nevada Department of Water Resources (NDWR) Department of Dam Safety.

Stage 4 construction was completed using the following documents:

- Drawings titled ACME Mining and Metals, ACME Tailings Impoundment, Stage 4 Construction Drawings, Conspiracy County, Nevada, Revision 0, dated May 13, 2010.
- Technical Specifications titled Technical Specifications for Construction, Stage 4 Expansion of the ACME Tailings Impoundment, dated May 13, 2010.

As-built drawings and as-built specifications are included in this report as Appendices A and B, respectively. All design clarifications made during Stage 3 construction have been incorporated into the as-built construction drawings and technical specifications. Design correspondence, including design clarifications and technical memorandums, are included in Appendix C. Results of geotechnical laboratory testing of soils are presented in Appendix D. Field density test results of soil materials are presented in Appendix E. Documentation for liner installation is presented in Appendix F. Daily Field Monitoring Reports are presented in Appendix G. In summary, the work completed for the Stage 4 expansion of the TSF was performed in general accordance with the Project Drawings and Technical Specifications, or in general accordance with engineer-approved revisions.

TRASH

Every word in the document should have a true, strong meaning.

There are many throw-away words in the English language that might sound fine if you are speaking, but which just clutter written documents without adding anything to meaning.

You can often delete them straight out, or replace three words with one, or replace with a shorter word.

If you find one case of a common "fat phrase" such as "in order to" in a document, use the search function to find all other cases of that word or phrase to delete or rewrite (you may decide to leave one or two cases, but 12 "in order to"s in a document is ridiculous).

Premium Tip

Additional Resources
More extensive lists can be found in "Client-Pleasing Reports and Communications" available on Amazon.com.

Deletable Trash

Some examples of words that you might often completely delete (because they add nothing, or not much, to the reader's understanding) include the following.

additionally	secondly	therefore	furthermore
in fact	as a matter of fact	on the basis of	with respect to
along the lines of	to a large extent	so to speak	that is to say that
note that	it is interesting that	importantly	

Redundancies

(using two words that mean the same thing, so your meaning repeats) can also be trimmed down. Here are some examples of redundancies.

combined total	close proximity	free gift	future forecast
young children	unexpected surprise	but however	commercial business
money-back refund	hushed silence	sorry tragedy	catastrophic disaster
added bonus	bare naked	end result	bond together
joint cooperation	lagging behind	and also	unique one of a kind
past history	forward planning	final conclusion	

ATM machine, PIN number, NDP party, CST tailings are also redundancies. The last letter of the abbreviation already stands for "machine," "number," "party," and "tailings."

Oxymorons

are silly combinations of words. They're more common than you think. Have you heard these combinations before?

friendly fire	elevated subway	intense apathy	original copies
business ethics	solid veneer	partial cease-fire	exact estimates
small crowd	non-dairy creamer	extensive briefing	unbiased opinion
taped live	open secret	pretty ugly	
standard options	alone together	limited lifetime guarantee	

Rewritable Trash

Jargon like "looking for synergies" and "paradigm shift" should be drop-kicked. Replace such nonsense with sentences that are concise and clear!

Wordy Phrases	Concise Phrase or Word
a majority of	most
a number of	many, several, some
a small number of	few
accounted for the fact that	because
along the lines	such as
are found to be, are known to be	are
as a consequence of	because
as per	per
as well as	and
at present, at the present time	now
at the time that	when
at this point in time	now
based on the fact that	because
by means of	by
despite the fact that	although
due to the fact that, due to	because, since
during the course of/during the time that	during, while
fewer in number	fewer
for the reason that	because
for the purpose of	to, for
has been shown to be	is
if it is assumed that	if
in length	long
in lieu of	instead of
in order to	to

Exercise 2: Empty the Trash

Use these strategies for this exercise:
- Shorten sentences.
- Put in active verbs.
- Use every day English.
- Make them more personal and direct.
- Cut out useless words.

1. The standing charge is payable in respect of each and every quarter.

2. You will be sent a letter regarding current charge rates not less often than once a year. Notice must be given of your intention to cancel the agreement a period of 30 days prior to your cancellation.

3. Should you be unable to agree to the contents of the statement or you have any questions thereon, please write to this department at the address overleaf, enclosing your passbook or certificate and the statement.

4. You are required to notify us immediately in the event of your unavoidable absence from work for sickness or any other reason and the attached note explains your obligations in this respect.

5. We would advise that attached herewith is the staff form which has been duly completed and would further advise that we should be grateful if you would give consideration to the various different documents to which we have made reference.

1.

2.

3.

4.

5.

"TO BE" VERBS: DANGEROUS BEINGS

The verb "to be" may be the easiest way to spot inefficient writing. Using this verb a few times is unavoidable, and just fine. The problems come when "to be" verbs travel in very large herds.

These monsters include is, was, are, were, been, being, have been, and has been.

Watch for these danger signals:
- "To be" verbs look as if they'd been applied to the page with a salt shaker.
- Two or more "to be" verbs show up in a single sentence.
- Two or more sentences in a row depend on "to be" as their primary verb.

Two categories of writing sin are committed with "to be" verbs. These are constructions commonly used in teaching English to ESL but can be refined down:
- equating sentences
- passive language

Both need attention.

Equating Sentences

Equating verbs equate. They do exactly the same thing as an equals sign in a formula.

And that's all they do, regardless of the complexity of the sentence or the thought that it contains.

Equating verbs tend to turn the action into a noun.

Somewhere in the sentence, you will usually find the real action disguised as a noun, sometimes as an adjective.

To get rid of a linking verb, turn the action back into a verb.

Instead of "My girl Mabel is a baseball player," write simply, "My girl Mabel plays baseball."

Instead of "Roger was a rider in the site truck that Aisha was a driver of," say

"Roger rode in the site truck that Aisha drove."

Exercise 3: Eliminate the Equations

Find the real action in these relatively simple examples. Get rid of the equating verb and make the real action verb take its proper place.

1. This action is a denial of human rights.

2. Your squad has always been the winner of intercollegiate competitions.

3. The report is an affirmation of your principles.

4. The poem was an explosion of energy.

5. The report is timely. It analyzes the totalitarian tendencies of the World Bank.

6. My aunt is an editor.

7. The intention of this report is to evaluate the benefits of rural gentrification.

1.

2.

3.

4.

5.

6.

7.

Passive Language

Where "to be" verbs appear, rewriting the sentence into an active form usually vastly reduces the number of words.

Active sentences are also much easier to read.

When you own up to your actions by saying "We collected the data" or "We wrote this report on time for you" it builds the relationship with the client.

Saying "the data was collected" is less useful in many ways:

1. We do not know who collected the data, which can be problematic in the future.

2. You miss a chance to build a relationship with the client.

3. Passively written sentences are always more drowsy-making and tedious to read.

Exercise 4: Activate the Passives

This is adapted from The United Church of Canada Pensions Department, but we generate many similar pieces of silliness in reports. How would you fix this?

Attached will be found an application form to be completed by persons who wish to have their payroll cheques deposited directly to the bank. The frequency or the time of the month at which cheques are issued will not be affected by the selection of this option. After selection, cheques will be deposited to an existing account or to a new account if that is desired. Receipt of this form is essential if this service is to be utilized. The application form can be easily completed. It is important to attach a sample cheque which has been marked "VOID."

Appendix I: Answers to Exercises

Exercise 1

BACKGROUND AND PROJECT DESCRIPTION This report documents construction activities and construction quality assurance (CQA) completed for the ACME Mine Tailings Storage Facility (TSF) expansion.

Project Description

ACME Mining and Metals (ACME) operates the ACME Mine located approximately 2 miles south of Area 51, in Conspiracy County, Nevada. The impoundment is operated by spigoting slurried fine mill tailings into the TSF using thin layer sub-aerial deposition to promote tailings drying and densification. The impoundment is a geomembrane-lined facility from which water is removed and recycled back to the mill for re-use.

The ACME TSF was designed to be constructed in seven stages. Stage 1 was substantially completed in December of 2005, Stage 2 was completed in September 2007, and Stage 3 was completed in November 2009. ACME completed construction of development Stages 4A and 4B, in September, 2011.

The Stage 4A expansion began in October 2009. This stage added approximately 3.0 million square feet of lined basin area to the existing TSF, and increased the dam height above the Stage 3 crest elevation by approximately 24 feet in the supernatant pool and transition areas. New embankment material was also added to the dam's west and east legs adjacent to the basin expansion .

Stage 4B construction followed Stage 4A construction with a winter shut-down during the 2010/2011 winter. The Stages 4A and 4B expansions combined added between approximately 30.4 million to 34.1 million tons of additional tailings storage capacity, with the range based on using either the originally assumed average density of 83 pounds per cubic foot (pcf) or a higher density of 93 pcf more recently inferred through surveys and field testing.

The key components constructed during Stage 4 included:

- construction of a staged temporary stormwater diversion ditch and retention pond north of the Stage 4 basin area
- the placement of earth and rock fill in the dam
- the installation of High Density polyethylene (HDPE) geomembrane liner in the impoundment basin area and upstream slope of the dam in the supernatant pool area
- the installation of the underdrain piping system above the HDPE liner system in the basin
- the extension of the gravity decant system on the upstream slope of the dam
- extensions to the crest drains on the additional embankment legs added on the east and west ends
- relocation of the tailings spigoting system from the Stage 3 to the Stage 4 dam crest and basin perimeter
- construction of the Stage 4 expansion occurred from June 2010 to September 2011.

Throughout this report, Stage 4 will refer to all work associated with both Stage 4A and Stage 4B. The dam and impoundment have been designed and constructed in accordance with Nevada Administrative Code (NAC) Chapter 445A and Water Pollution Control Permit NEV-0000 as administered by the Nevada Division of Environmental Protection (NDEP) Bureau of Mining Regulation and Reclamation, and in accordance with NAC Chapter 535 and Dam Permit J-000 as administered by the Nevada Department of Water Resources (NDWR) Department of Dam Safety.

The following documents were used during Stage 4 construction:

- Drawings titled ACME Mining and Metals, ACME Tailings Impoundment, Stage 4 Construction Drawings, Conspiracy County, Nevada, Revision 0, dated May 13, 2010

- Technical Specifications titled Technical Specifications for Construction, Stage 4 Expansion of the ACME Tailings Impoundment, dated May 13, 2010

The attached Appendices include the following:

- Appendix A: As-built drawings, including design clarifications made during Stage 3 construction

- Appendix B: As-built specifications, including design clarifications made during Stage 3 construction

- Appendix C: Design correspondence, including design clarifications and technical memorandums

- Appendix D: Results from the geotechnical laboratory soil testing

- Appendix E: Field soil density test results

- Appendix F: Documentation for liner installation

- Appendix G: Daily Field Monitoring Reports

In summary, the TSF Stage 4 expansion work was performed in general accordance with the Project Drawings and Technical Specifications, or in general accordance with engineer-approved revisions.

Exercise 2

1. The standing charge is payable each quarter.

2. You will be sent a letter about current charge rates once a year. Thirty days' written notice must be given to cancel the agreement.

3. If you disagree with or have questions about the statement, please write to this department at the address overleaf. Enclose your passbook or certificate and the statement.

4. Please notify us immediately when you will be absent from work, as described in the policy.

5. Please see the completed staff form and the referenced documents.

Exercise 3

1. This action denies human rights.

2. Your squad always wins intercollegiate competitions.

3. The report affirms your principles.

4. The poem exploded with energy.

5. This timely report analyzes the totalitarian tendencies of the World Bank.

6. My aunt edits.

7. This report intends to evaluate the benefits of rural gentrification.

Exercise 4

Complete the attached application form to have your payroll cheques deposited directly to your bank. Attach a sample cheque marked "VOID." The timing of your payments will remain the same whether you choose to receive cheques or use direct deposit.

Appendix II: Team Troubleshooting Strategies

A Note on Giving Feedback

Professional colleagues, especially international ones who are learning English as a second, third, or even fourth or fifth language, are often interested in professional development and willing to improve their writing. If seniors, or language reviewers, can take the time to make explanatory comments to send back to these writers, they can learn and improve. I have seen some excellent improvement in just months or a year with some people.

I have also heard many rants from people who get tired of fixing the English of their co-workers, and who perceive that certain co-workers are not trying hard enough. Be realistic. Identify what the issues really are – is there actual laziness occurring, or is the person doing their best, but perhaps dealing with too heavy a load? Or, is the feedback that they are receiving perhaps not clear enough?

If team members are frustrated, try to find out, are they giving useful feedback? Or are they asking for changes in a way that the person receiving the requests can not process? It is useful to take a step back and assess this.

Sometimes thoughtful language tutoring through review by someone outside your group, someone who will make considered comments, can succeed if you are frustrated with improving a particular writer.

Many group managers also succeed in helping their people write better by the same method, of course! Some tips:

- Use praise for things done right.
- When you make a correction, explain the linguistic reason for the correction.
- Invite the person receiving the feedback to an in-person meeting if possible.
- If time permits, show other examples of a certain type of error they are struggling with.
- If time permits, correct one case (for example, using plural forms as adjectives, such as "the drills stems" instead of "the drill stems") and explain it, then get them to return to their work and correct other cases before you continue to edit the report.

Premium Tip

What Managers Can Do: Improving Writing Quality in Your Group

Document quality can not improve if your writers are not willing members of the process. The table on the next page decribes some psychological reasons and solutions that are not usually discussed aloud in consulting firms, but which are useful to consider for managers who want to effect change.

The willingness of colleagues to accept feedback has many causes:	How Leaders Can Help
1. **Their own self-confidence level.** Paradoxically, people who come across as arrogantly unwilling to accept input are actually often the ones who are afraid to admit they are less than perfect. The number one reason (from my observations) that people at work refuse to incorporate others' feedback is a worried feeling that if they don't do it all themselves, others will judge them. In truth, the most confident, high-level, successful colleagues are usually open to at least discussing input, even if they disagree. And successful, confident people are usually happy to make changes when they receive good suggestions for improvement.	Make people feel comfortable with doing teamwork. Praise and promote those who use the team structure properly and respectfully. Make language review mandatory, so that people do not have to self-judge in order to seek help. Connect people with a mentor, so they can discuss their needs confidentially and get better within comfort zones.
2. **Time pressures.** People who feel stressed and overloaded may not feel that they have time to incorporate feedback.	Develop schedules with your team that incorporate sufficient time for a language review step. Insist that team members meet the schedule – do not allow team members to trim the language revision step.
3. **Respect for the reviewer and/or the feedback they offer.** An example of this that I have sadly seen too often is people who "do language editing" but are making errors, or are making unnecessary changes. These actions do not inspire confidence and can cause tension in a team.	Do not assume that, for example, if someone is in a senior admin role, or an intermediate science role, they will be a good language reviewer. Assess the skills of people on your team and assign tasks appropriately.

AUTHOR BIO

Christa Bedwin has 18 years of experience writing, editing, and teaching in industry, government, academia, and educational publishing.

She now teaches engineers, scientists, and business people to communicate better, and helps people to publish books to preserve their knowledge and wisdom.

Christa was raised on a ranch in the foothills of the Rockies and has travelled extensively. She has a wide range of job and crazy travel experiences and is a dynamic instructor and speaker. Her positive attitude and enthusiasm are contagious.

www.ingramcontent.com/pod-product-compliance
Lightning Source LLC
Chambersburg PA
CBHW051431200326
41520CB00023B/7430